Chowdaheadz

A WICKED SMAAHT GUIDE
TO ALL THINGS
BOSTON

Chowdaheadz

A WICKED SMAAHT GUIDE TO ALL THINGS BOSTON

RYAN DeLISLE &
RYAN GORMADY

ILLUSTRATIONS
BY KEVIN MULKERN

Globe
Pequot

GUILFORD, CONNECTICUT

Globe
Pequot

An imprint of Rowman & Littlefield

Distributed by NATIONAL BOOK NETWORK

British Library Cataloguing in Publication Information available

Library of Congress Cataloging-in-Publication Data available

ISBN (paperback) 978-1-4930-2477-3
ISBN (e-book) 978-1-4930-2478-0

♾™ The paper used in this publication meets the minimum requirements of American National Standard for Information Sciences—Permanence of Paper for Printed Library Materials, ANSI/NISO Z39.48-1992.

Printed in the United States

Contents

What the Heck is a Chowdahead?. vii

Wicked Weather. 1

The Geography of Boston 13

Food & Drink 41

Traffic & Transportation 87

Whadjasay 109

Sports 173

Index. 195

About the Authors. 199

What the Heck is a Chowdahead?

A Chowdahead is someone who lives, or has lived, in Boston and maintains a wicked big sense of regional pride. We believe Boston is the best place to live and are fanatical about our sports teams. Most of the loud-mouthed, crude, fast-driving, New England accent, binge drinking stereotypes are true and we wouldn't want it any other way.

Whether you've been to Boston once, lived here your entire life, or just plan to visit one day, Boston has a lot of universal references throughout pop culture. This book is the go-to resource for people to learn, get a laugh, and understand the people of Boston. FYI: No locals call Boston "Beantown."

Wicked Weather

"If you don't like the weather in New England, wait a minute."

—MARK TWAIN

Whether it's the No Name Storm, the Blizzard of '78, or just a typical spring day of heat in the morning and A/C at night, the weather in Boston is undoubtedly always a topic of conversation. We take the art of wearing layers to a whole new level. There are three seasons "winter," "almost winter," and "It's too hot." People generally start saying, "Summer is over" in mid-July. And allergies are always "bad this year."

Foliage

There's a saying in Boston that "October is my favorite color" because the leaves around here are like nowhere else. In fact, New England is the only place that has red leaves in their foliage variety. People come from all over the world to see them. These people are known as **"Leaf Peepahs."** They drive the roads of New England just to enjoy the breathtaking scenery while it lasts.

The leaves changing is a major part of life in Boston; it sets the background for the last few weeks of "non-wintah." The abundance of leaves doesn't come without a lot of work for homeowners though, who tend to hate the cleanup caused by fall.

Heat Wave

Though we complain about the winter all year, people in Boston still love to complain about the heat. There is a difference between an isolated scorchah and an official heat wave. In order for it to be official, there needs to be three consecutive days over 90 degrees.

Though a full week of 87- and 88-degree days may be too hot for some people, it's not a heat wave.

Since much of Boston was built before central air conditioning was a thing, we have to rely on our window units and fans to keep us cool and sane during the heat wave. Unless you know someone with a pool, you're most likely going to be cooling down at Castle Island or Revere Beach.

Indian Summah

People in Boston tend to think summah ends the third week of August when kids and teachers alike begin to get in their school routine and Dunks starts rolling out their pumpkin spice lattes; however, fall doesn't officially begin until the end of September.

Indian summah is when the city experiences an unseasonably warm day in the fall. It can't officially be an Indian summah unless two things happen: it's during the season of fall and there has already been the first frost. Because these two factors need to occur, an Indian summah day is rare, but typically happens in late October or November.

Muggy

The humidity in Boston is unlike anywhere else; so when the temperature is 86 degrees with 100 percent humidity, it can feel almost 100 degrees. There is no denying when it's a muggy day; it's so unpleasant that you feel "mugged" when you open the door to step outside. If your legs have ever stuck to a chair when you try to get up, then you've experienced "muggy-like" conditions.

Nor'Eastah

New England has interesting weather all year long. Unique to the Northeast are Nor'Eastahs! These macro-scale cyclones get their name from the direction of their winds, which blow from over the North Atlantic Ocean. The time of year it occurs determines if it will bring rain or snow—usually in excess. When we get a rainy Nor'Eastah, you'll hear Bostonians all over say, "At least it's not snow!"

No Name Storm

Sometimes a Nor'Eastah comes from the north and collides with a storm from the south, which create a storm you can only find in New England. In 1993, the Massachusetts coast saw one of its most epic storms in modern history. The storm, known around here as "the No Name Storm" was famously depicted in the movie, *The Perfect Storm*. It was called the No Name Storm because it was the combination of two storms, none of which were hurricanes, so it didn't get named by the National Weather Service.

The storm hit Massachusetts on Halloween and much of the coastline from Maine down was forced to evacuate. The crazy part was that towns on the coast were hit very hard and towns inland felt minimal effects. Whether you felt it or not, the storm caused over $200 million in damage and killed thirteen people.

Scorchah

Around the end of May when kids are still in school, the first hot days bring excitement and a preview of what summer is going to be like. These days, especially the first ones, are what we call "Scorchahs." Other parts of the world may call it a scorcher, a reference to something hot; but in Boston, it's a scorchah. Even the meteorologists use this lingo because they know it's the only way to make their point.

"It's going to be a scorchah today, stay hydrated!"

Response: "Oh ya!"

Wintah

Though winter is officially from December 21st through March 20th, wintah is from Halloween to Easter and is the topic of conversation all year long. The lingering memories from winters past are prevalent in people's minds even when they're at the beach or enjoying a 4th of July BBQ because they know it's coming. This fear is what makes Bostonians active the whole rest of the year. Cramming birthday parties, christenings, dinners, and any other live event, into the months of "non wintah."

Some Bostonians and New Englanders are famous for their winter amnesia. During non wintah, we forget just how bad the previous winter was and how bad it will get again. In the dead of summer people truly block it out in order to justify why they still live in the greatest city in the United States.

Blizzard of '78

Boston experienced one of the worst storms in history in 1978 and anyone who was lived through it will tell you all about it, and probably has . . . ad nauseum. Bostonians make reference to the Blizzard of '78 more than anything else (except maybe the Big Dig). One of the reasons it impacted the city, and surrounding areas, so much is that it was not forecasted as precisely as they're able to do today. People were literally stuck in cars on the highways; over 3,500 abandoned cars would be found on highways during the clean up. Only emergency personnel were allowed to leave their homes. Even though we broke the snowfall record in 2015, Bostonians will still talk about the Blizzard of '78 forever.

The Geography of Boston

Bostonians may come across as a united front, but underneath it all, we take where we come from very serious. Someone from East Boston would be mad if they were mistaken to be from South Boston (when they're essentially the same place to an outsider).

Boston is located in the commonwealth of Massachusetts, is the largest city in New England, and is best known for inventing America. Though we are not the biggest in the United States, our words and traditions continually leave their mark on pop culture worldwide. No matter where you go, when you say you're from Boston, the people you meet will all have an idea of who you are and how you talk.

Massachusetts is a Commonwealth; Not a State

What does this mean besides elected officials just using the word "commonwealth" when most others say "state?" A commonwealth is a designated territory ruled by the people, not the government; essentially why the United States declared independence from the British to begin with. There are only four commonwealths in the United States: Massachusetts, Pennsylvania, Virginia and Kentucky.

The first three (Massachusetts, Pennsylvania, and Virginia) date back to their early succession from Britain; while Kentucky is simply because it used to be part of Virginia until the Civil War, but still remained a commonwealth. The designation of commonwealth has no legal standing, but it's still cool; and now you know what it means when someone asks!

COMMONWEALTH (NOT STATE)

OF MASSACHUSETTS

NOT A STATE

ENSE PETIT PLACIDAM SVB LIBERTATE QVIETEM

CHARLES-TOWN
EAST BOSTON
NORTH END
ALLSTON-BRIGHTON
BACK BAY
BEACON HILL
CENTRAL
FEN-WAY/KENMORE
BROOKLINE
SOUTH END
SOUTHIE
JAMAICA PLAIN
ROXBURY
DORCHESTER
WEST ROX-BURY
ROSLINDALE
MATTA PAN
HYDE PARK

Neighborhoods & Favorites Areas

According to a studies, most Bostonians have differing opinions about where a neighborhood starts and ends. The inconsistencies in zip codes, parking restrictions, and Realtor definitions make it hard to tell who is right and who is wrong. Your Realtor may tell you that your apartment is in the Southie to appease your requests; while the neighbors consider it Dorchester. Further, you could have a South Boston resident parking sticker but have a Dorchester zip code—so who is right?

Some neighborhoods, like The North End and East Boston, are easier to define than others like Allston/Brighton due to natural borders. Also, in a city of recent redevelopment and growth, there are new neighborhoods coming and going constantly. (Remember the West End?) Is "The Seaport" part of "Southie" or is its part of Downtown's Waterfront? Some would refer to it as "South Boston" to differentiate from "Southie." (Neither of which should be confused with the South End.)

My East Boston neighborhood was not in question since it has Boston Harbor as a natural boundary; however tell an Eastie resident who lives in the Jeffries Point neighborhood that he lives in Orient Heights, and he'll have no problem correcting you. So is my neighborhood East Boston or Jeffries Point?

At the end of the day, we're all Bostonians but what makes our city great is the differences in neighborhoods!

The Back Bay

The Back Bay is one of the most prestigious neighborhoods in Boston and is also recognized as one of the best-preserved examples of nineteenth-century urban architecture in the United States. It's also home to some of the most architecturally significant buildings in the city, such as the Boston Public Library. The neighborhood is an international shopping Mecca; including the trendy Newbury St. and Boylston St. as well as many of Boston's tallest buildings.

Beacon Hill

The neighborhood, referred to by locals as "The Hill," is located between Boston Common, the Charles River, and Cambridge Street. Given its proximity to the hustle and bustle of downtown and the Back Bay, it is unusually quiet; most likely due to the brick homes shielding the area from traffic noise. The most expensive part of the city, and possibly the country, is located in the center of Beacon Hill called Louisburg Square. It's home to John Kerry, the Kennedys, and other prominent figures. To the square's left, is Acorn Street which is also known as "the most frequently photographed street in the United States."

If you take a trip to Boston, you'll most likely end up in Boston Common. I highly recommend taking the extra ten-minute walk over to Beacon Hill. No matter season, you'll instantly fall in love with the charm of the area. There isn't much to do (which is what makes it great), so bring your camera and take it all in. Stop in some of the shops and grab a slice of pizza (we recommend Nino's!), you'll be glad you did!

Charlestown

Charlestown is one the oldest neighborhoods in the country and with only 1 square mile, it's filled with history! Home to the U.S.S. *Constitution* (Old Ironsides), this waterfront neighborhood has a lot to see and do. In recent years, the neighborhood has become popular for urban professionals who love the proximity to downtown, the waterfront, and the charm of the architecture and narrow streets.

Dorchester

Dorchester is located south of downtown Boston, is the biggest neighborhood in Boston proper. The neighborhood is divided by Dorchester Avenue. Given its 6 square-mile size, it is home to much diversity. What was once an English settlement is now the home to a large African American and Asian population.

East Boston

When people think of East Boston, they most likely think of Logan Airport or the place where a casino was supposed to go. Often times, people don't think of it as a Boston neighborhood; even though "Boston" is half of its namesake. Separated from the rest of the city by Boston Harbor, Eastie offers many reasons you should jump in the tunnel and check out all it has to offer! Given its proximity to the harbor and downtown, it makes for the best views of Boston's skyline; night or day!

Jamaica Plain

By far the most green part of Boston (not the green you'd likely associate with the other Jamaica), Jamaica Plain, or JP, has tons of parks, the Arnold Arboretum, and the Jamaica Way all appealing to Bostonians who enjoy outdoor activities.

The 4.4-square-mile neighborhood located just south of Fenway is very diverse and filled with lots of artsy people who care about their community and well-being.

North End

The North End is one of Boston's (America's!) oldest continually inhabited neighborhoods. Dating back to the 1630s, it is also one Boston's smallest neighborhoods, measuring only .36 square miles. It may be small, but there is a ton to do (eat) there and it is full of rich history! Mostly populated by Italian-Americans, it is known for some of the best food in the city! Anywhere you stand in the North End, you can see, and smell, an Italian restaurant, bakery, or cafe and they're all always busy no matter what time of day you go! Walking down the crooked narrow streets will make you feel like you're in Italy, not Boston. If you want the perfect night out, grab your favorite pasta dish at any restaurant then walk over to a pastry shop for dessert and follow it up at a cozy wine/cigar bar—you'll be so happy you did!

Rozzie

Roslindale, or "Rozzie" is the most suburban neighborhood in Boston. Roslindale Village is the heart of the neighborhood and everything revolves around it. It is located on the commuter line so it is a very popular spot for Bostonians to raise families while still commuting to their jobs downtown.

South End

Not to be confused with Southie, the South End District of Boston is one of the best places in town for architecture, restaurants, and music. Nestled between The Back Bay, South Boston, Roxbury, and Dorchester this part of the city is not south of downtown at all; which with most of Boston neighborhoods, doesn't make sense.

Southie

When most people hear South Boston they think of Whitey Bulger and Martin Scorsese movies like *The Departed*. Those thoughts may have applied a few decades ago but now South Boston is "Southie" and everyone wants a piece of it! What started out as a "cheap place to live" has morphed into an urban mecca of which twenty- to thirty-year-olds can't get enough. Boston has always had a large amount of young people due to the fact we are the home to so many colleges and universities. Once people get a taste of it here, they don't want to leave—and who can blame them?

ZooMass

Massachusetts is home to many colleges, especially in the Boston area, but none of them are quite as infamous for their parties as UMASS Amherst. The flagship of the University of Massachusetts schools earned its nickname of "Zoo Mass" or "The Zoo" in the seventies when it seemed to have no rules. The nickname and reputation live on; it was ranked the #7 party school in the nation in 2013 and the #1 party school in Massachusetts in 2014.

UMASS students and alum take pride in their partying capabilities and even more pride in the nickname.

Boston Common

Boston Common is the oldest public city park in the United States, dating back to 1634. One can tell a true Bostonian from tourist when the tourist says, "Boston CommonS." Given its age, the park has a long history. The Common was once used as a battleground in the Revolution then later was the site of cattle grazing for families around Boston.

It is located in front of the Massachusetts State House, making it the home to many rallies and protests. Including a frog pond in the middle and large sections of grass, you never know what you'll see walking through "The Common."

Boston Gas Tank

If you've commuted into Boston by car or on the Red Line, or sat in Cape traffic on the Southeast Expressway, you've seen the Boston Gas tank painted with a rainbow swash. The tank was painted in 1971 and moved to its current location in 1992. The design was made by Corita Kent in an 8-inch scale that was adapted to the current 140-foot design it is today. Most people who pass it reference the "Asian Man" in the blue stripe; who is believed to be Ho Chi Min; the leader of Vietnam in protest to the war (though King denies that it is in fact him). Another notable celebrity in the design is Fred Flinstone who is supposedly looking southward in the yellow strip. The design is the largest copyrighted work of art in the world.

Faneuil Hall

Located across from Boston's waterfront, nestled between the North End and Chinatown, Faneuil Hall is a must visit for tourists and locals alike. It was the first public outdoor market of its kind and still operates as the home to many small local merchants. There is something for everyone to do in Faneuil Hall. Grab a pint at the Black Rose while taking in some Irish music or have some chowdah in the upstairs food court. You will also see street performers and historic reenactments while being surrounded by beautiful historic buildings.

Hancock Tower

The second John Hancock Tower (known by locals as the "Old Hancock Tower") was built in 1947. At the time, it was the second tallest building in the city; only 1 foot shorter than the Custom House tower in Faneuil Hall. The building sits in the heart of the Back Bay and is distinguishable in Boston's skyline.

The top of the Old Hancock is home to the Berkeley Weather Beacon, which uses lights to alert the city of current and upcoming weather. Here is a poem to remember what the colors mean:

Steady blue, clear view
Flashing blue, clouds due
Steady red, storms ahead
Flashing red, snow instead

During baseball season, it also lets the city know if the game is rained out. So you should always take a minute to look up and see what's going on!

Haymarket

Haymarket is an open-air market located next to Faneuil Hall and the North End and has been operating since 1830. The market sells fruits, vegetables, and other produce at a much cheaper price than a supermarket. The market is only open two days a week, Friday and Saturday, so when it is open, it's packed.

The Hub

The hub is actually short for "The Hub of the Solar System" and it refers specifically to the Massachusetts State House. The golden-domed building got this nickname in 1858 from Oliver Wendell Holmes. He wrote in an article, "[The] Boston State-House is the hub of the solar system. You couldn't pry that out of a Boston man, if you had the tire of all creation straightened out for a crowbar." This implies that Boston is the center of the universe; which can only mean that Bostonian's Masshole attitude dates all the way back to the 1800's. . . . sounds about right!

Though most people don't know the origin of the nickname (until now!), it is still often used around the world when people refer to Boston. It's used during sporting events as a synonym for Boston much like New York would be "The Big Apple." There's also the famous restaurant at the top of the Prudential Center called "Top of the Hub" because it's located at one of the highest points in Boston.

Newbury Street

Newbury Street was one of the earliest roads in Boston, named after the Battle of Newbury. The street, adorned with brownstones, runs east to west through the heart of the Back Bay connecting Boston Common to Mass Avenue. It is now a shopping mecca to people from around the world. Though it is known for its high-end boutiques and posh surroundings, Newbury Street has shops and restaurants that cater to everyone.

Massachusetts Bay

Cape Cod Bay

Buzzards Bay

Why is Massachusetts Called the Bay State?

The answer probably isn't what you expected! Most Bostonians would guess that Massachusetts has this nickname simply because it's a coastal state and there are a lot of bays; however, it's not that simple.

According to WiseGeek.com, there are two theories about the nickname's origin. The first is because the Pilgrims settled on Cape Cod Bay. The second theory is a little more interesting. The company that was granted a British Royal Charter to populate the new colonies was called The Massachusetts Bay Company. The Bay Company governed the colonies, now known as New England, from 1629 to 1684.

So if the second theory is true, it would infer that "Bay" doesn't have anything to do with bodies of water, but with a company/charter that includes the name "Bay" in it.

I've lived in Massachusetts for thirty-two years and had no idea about the second theory; I always assumed it was because there are a lot of bays . . . hope you found this interesting. Who knows, maybe you'll be asked this on *Jeopardy* someday!

Down The Cape

Every summer, people from all over the world flock to one of the greatest places on the planet: Cape Cod. Many Bostonians are lucky enough to have a house down there or the second best option—a friend with a house down there. You can tell a Bostonian on the Cape versus a non-Bostonian because we don't say "I'm going to Cape Cod;" we say, "I'll be down the Cape."

The Cape is a man-made peninsula in Massachusetts connected to the mainland by two bridges; the Sagamore and Bourne. You'll often hear people say, "bridge traffic" and use "the rotary" as an indicator. "Bridge traffic was backed up 6 miles from the rotary." Or "It took me four hours to get off the Cape last weekend." People sit in hours of traffic every Friday and Sunday, so it must be special.

Home to some of the best beaches on the East Coast; with spectacular sand dunes throughout, Cape Cod is the place to be a beach bum. In addition to the beaches, there are a multitude of mini golf courses and the best lobstah rolls you'll find anywhere. From Provincetown to Falmouth; you're sure to find something to make your summer wicked awesome.

The Islands

In addition to the Cape, Bostonians also have the option to visit "The Islands,"—Martha's Vineyard and Nantucket. Like any island, they're only accessible by plane or boat; which makes them quite exclusive. Martha's Vineyard, or "The Vineyard," is located 3 miles off of Cape Cod and was famously featured in the movie *Jaws*. Despite its name, there are no active commercial vineyards. The island is 100 square miles and is known for being an affluent summer destination. Nantucket, or "ACK," is located 30 miles south of Cape Cod. Since Nantucket is a little farther away than the Vineyard, it has always been a little more exclusive.

Food & Drink

In Boston we have two food groups, "Dunks" & everything else. The everything else includes some very notable things; from marshmallow creme to seafood, Bostonians know how to eat. Whether you're dining at a BBQ in your neighbor's yard or at a spinning restaurant above town, you're going to eat well.

Keggah

Bostonians don't go to keg parties, we go to keggahs. Whether you're at your local frat house or down the Cape for the summah, chances are you'll be going to a keggah. Most keggahs have cheap beer to fill the cups needed for Beirut (not beer pong!) or to do your standard keg stand. While beer is usually cheap (we save the Sam Adams for big occasions), by the end of the keggah, it all tastes the same. If you're throwing a keggah, you always want to be sure and have some extra **thirty racks** for when the keg is **kicked**. Whether it's the high-quality stuff or cheap beer, you're sure to save the day with a **thirty rack**. You can always tell who went to UMASS (see: Zoo Mass) because they share a **thirty rack** between two people, three during desperate times; while the Boston College kids can share one between five or six people and get **plastahed**.

Frappe

On a hot summer day there is nothing better than enjoying a frappe at your favorite ice cream place. A frappe is very different than a milkshake. Okay not really, it's a milkshake with ice cream. A frappe consists of milk, ice cream, and flavor syrup that is blended or whipped until foamy. Our neighbors to the south in Rhode Island call it a "cabinet" and we aren't sure why.

Fluff

Fluff is a creation of marshmallow creme that originated just outside of Boston, in Somerville, Massachusetts. It is one of the essential ingredients for a fluffahnuttah sandwich; put some fluff and peanut butter between two slices of white bread and you'll have a wicked good sandwich! Forget the jelly, that's for English muffins. There isn't a kid's sandwich more Bostonian than a fluffahnuttah!

Badaydahs

Potatoes have been a staple in Boston dishes ever since the influx of Irish emigrants to the city. Whether they're mashed, fried, scalloped, roasted, seared, you are almost certain to have potatoes with every meal. You name it, there's nothing better than some meat and badaydahs for suppah!

Bubblah

In Boston we refer to water fountains as Bubblahs because the water bubbles from the spout. A fountain is what you see in the park, or in front of a rich person's house. Bubbler used to be the brand name of a certain kind of water fountain and the name stuck in Boston. If you're looking for a drink of cold water during a scorchah, don't ask for a water fountain unless you plan on going for a swim.

Chowdah

Chowdah is a creamy milk-based broth soup with clams or other seafood and lots of butter. Garnish that with some oyster crackers or Saltines and you've got yourself the greatest thing God invented. No matter where you go in Boston, they're going to tell you they have the best clam chowdah in town, and they're probably right! It's hard to find a bad clam chowder. Unless of course you're in New York where they haven't learned that it's NOT tomato–based.

Cuppah Regulah

Other coffee chains use funny words when it comes to ordering coffee drinks, but Boston only has one. When you order a "regulah" coffee, it is going to have cream and sugar in it; two of each to be exact. So don't make the mistake of thinking you'll get a black coffee with nothing in it. What's so confusing about that? Though Dunks reigns supreme when it comes to coffee, a cuppah regulah is universal in any coffee shop around Boston.

Dunks

What started out as a single donut shop in Quincy, Massachusetts, in 1950 has morphed into a Massachusetts icon. You can drive five minutes (err three minutes) in any direction in Boston and find at least one Dunkin Donuts. You can usually stand at one and see another. The endless drive-through lines at every location at any given hour prove that Boston runs on Dunkin. The rest of the country must think Bostonians are fat based on how much we talk about "donuts," when in reality, we are talking about their coffee. That's not to say that their doughy goodness goes unnoticed. Everyone needs a crullah or munchkin every now and again.

Cod

Though cod is a popular fish off of New England's shores (see: Cape Cod), it's also an acronym in other parts of the world for "Catch of the Day." In New England, however, we use the term *Scrod* for that. Scrod is the white fish of the day on the menu; which is typically young cod fish . . . get it?

Cranberries

One of the only native fruits to Massachusetts, cranberries are a huge industry in the Bay State. The bright red fruits have been deemed a "super food" for their unique nutrient content and antioxidants. They are grown in bogs that are flooded with water to harvest. This timeless process is still very much part of life in the southeastern part of Massachusetts and Cape Cod. They are a staple on Thanksgiving tables across the United States in so many different forms.

Franks and Beans

There's an old New England tradition of having franks and beans on Saturday nights. The meal is just as it sounds, beans and hot dogs. People have their own variations of how to make the perfect beans, but regardless of the method, this Saturday tradition happens at town halls, masonic lodges, and churches all over New England. There are many stories behind how this tradition came about, but the most common is that the early Boston colonists made it on Saturday because it would keep overnight and they could have it Sunday too; which was a sacred day of rest.

Hoodsie

Hoodsie Cups are little pieces of heaven in cardboard dishes with their own little spoons. Not only are they the perfect size, they also settle the internal debate of "chocolate or vanilla" by offering both! Whether you're at Fenway Park or at your local ice cream truck, you can't go wrong with this refreshing treat.

Italian Ice

If you're looking to cool off on a hot day, you're going to need some Italian ice. It's a sweetened frozen concoction made with fruit and flavoring. They can be found all over New England in the summer months; oftentimes operating from a push cart. The two flavors you can always find are lemon and watermelon. If you find one that is root bee-ah flavored, you've hit the jackpot!

Jimmies

The chocolate things you put on top of an ice cream cone; not to be confused with rainbow sprinkles! Some people think the term is racist, but that has since been proven false. When you're traveling around the country and ask for jimmies, don't be surprised if the ice cream scooper looks at you funny and has no idea what you mean!

Lobstah Roll

Nothing says summah in Boston like a lobstah roll; a lobster meat sandwich soaked in butter served in a grilled hot dog bun (mayo and celery are optional.) They're often served with chips or french fries depending on if you plan to eat it then or later. It's rare to go to a restaurant in Boston, or New England for that matter, without seeing a lobstah roll on the menu. They're often the most expensive sandwich offered, but worth every penny.

Market Basket

People in and around Boston take their grocery prices very serious. Everyone knows that prices can't be beat at Market Basket. The old timers still refer to it as DeMoula's and the people around here will do just about anything to defend the DeMoula name. In 2014, the (non-union) employees striked to save their beloved CEO, and oust his cousin with the same name, and the loyal patrons of Market Basket followed suit.

Necco

New England Confectionary Candy Company. Those candy hearts that everyone hates to love on Valentine's Day have been part of American culture since 1902. The company is still thriving in Revere, Massachusetts. Though they're most famous for the candy hearts, they also make a wafer that can be found in every grocery store. The candies are 90% sugar and 80% likely to chip your teeth, but so worth it.

Sub

Not be confused with a replacement teacher while yours is out sick, "sub" is short for submarine sandwich. Though the origin is unknown, it is believed to have originated in New London, Connecticut, during World War II. It's a sandwich in a long roll.

Boston has a sub shop on every corner. You can also get a sub at any pizza shop (also on every corner). In addition to the sub shops and pizza places, the north shore also has a plethora of roast beef places. Though Kelly's Roast Beef is the most famous, there is no shortage of just as good places. Most Bostonians don't know this isn't the case everywhere else, but we love us a good roast beef sub!

Pahdee Plattah

Long before people started putting kale in their smoothies and making kale chips they found on Pinterest, it used to be the tasteless garnish on the bottom of a Pahdee Plattah. Whether it's Johnny's christening or Pauly's first communion, chances are there is going to be a platter with cold cuts and cheeses for you to make your own subs. Available at any sub shop, these meat-filled trays have been a staple at Boston gatherings forever.

Tonic

The midwest has always called it "pop" and the south "coke," and everywhere in the northeast, besides Boston, it is referred to as "soda." In Boston, it has always been tonic. If you ask for a tonic in Boston you better mean a Coke or Pepsi, not that clear liquid with water bubbles that makes you burp. Sit down and have a swig of tonic with your lobstah roll!

New England Boiled Dinnah

New England boiled dinner is a huge tradition on St. Patrick's Day for Irish and non-Irish alike. Its simpler term is "corned beef and cabbage." The meal consists of corned beef, cabbage, and other variations of vegetables; most common being carrots, potato and white turnips.

Ireland produced a lot of the meat in the Atlantic trade from cattle, in fact it was half of Ireland's exports in the late 1600s. Most people in Ireland did not eat the beef product because it was too expensive, plus, it was more valuable to export. Ironically, corned beef was looked down upon in the (now US) colonies because it was associated with poverty.

American families all have their own recipes and traditions with regard to preparing their boiled dinner. Aside from cutting up the vegetables, the meal is quite simple to make. Some serve it with mustard and others with vinegar. Some boil in beer and others water or variation of the two. The meal takes all day to make and will make your whole house smell delicious, so that smell is clearly associated with the holiday.

Though people who like boiled dinner tend to *love* boiled dinner, it's not usually served any other day of the year.

My family boils our dinner in equal parts water and beer on a slow heat and includes: corned beef, carrots, unpeeled potatoes, and cabbage. I, for one, cannot get enough! I always have big plans for corned beef sandwiches the rest of the week but that rarely happens because it's all gone in a fraction of the time it takes to prepare.

Dinner vs Supper

If you're from Boston you've definitely heard your mom tell you to "be home for suppah," and "set the table for dinner," but have you ever wondered what the difference is? Supper or suppah is a less-formal, light meal served before or after dinner, if dinner was in the afternoon or late in the evening. Dinner is the main meal of the day or an event. So you have suppah at the kitchen table before homework and dinnah in the dining room on Sunday with the whole family.

Traffic & Transportation

When traveling in Boston, you may be driving north on one highway and south on the other without even knowing or you might go around in endless circles if you aren't paying attention in a rotary. If you don't feel like driving, get your Charlie card and let the T do all the work. Whatever you do, just don't ask for directions (see the Dunkin Donuts section).

Bang a Uey

With all the roadwork in the Boston area (the Big Dig, uh hum), there is a constant uncertainty of how to get places. When one is going in the wrong direction, they don't simply "turn around," or "make a u-turn," they "Bang a Uey." One usually bangs a uey with some fear and a lot of gusto, as their time is limited and Bostonians don't mess around when it comes to driving.

Beatah

Most us of have had them, and we've definitely all seen them. You know, those cars next to you at the red light that are just trying to make it to the next red light. In Boston we call them "beatahs" because they've certainly been beaten over time.

Big Dig

Not only was the Big Dig the biggest civil engineering project in the history of the world; it's also what Bostonians love to talk about when there's nothing else to talk about. (Take note tourists!) Since the roads in Boston were built for horse and buggy and we are in a world of automobiles, the city had a major traffic problem that was only going to get worse. The major obstacles the city faced were lack of space and access to the airport.

The solution: Put the central artery underground and build a second tunnel. Before the big dig, the city had a second, much uglier, green monster running through downtown, blocking off access to the waterfront. This monstrosity was a six-lane freeway used every day, all day, known as the central artery.

Engineers had to figure out a way to build this underground tunnell while still allowing people to commute every day. Needless to say, they faced some obstacles. . . and budget problems, but the Big Dig officially ended in 2003 when the Ted Williams Tunnell opened, connecting the Mass Pike to Logan Airport.

Though people like to (still) complain about the Big Dig, it essentially shaped the city for the better. The second green monster is gone and was replaced with a park, The Rose Kennedy Greenway, that runs through all of downtown complete with art installations and carousels. People can now access the waterfront and North End by foot. There is now two ways to access the airport traffic without adding to downtown traffic.

Blinkahs

Though not often used in the greater Boston area, blinkahs let other drivers around you know which direction you're turning or on which side you're about to cut them off (the latter being more often). Some parts of the world call them directionals, which is just downright weird; while others call them turn signals, which takes way too long. So blinkahs is clearly the only way. Don't be wicked lame, use yah blinkahs!

Breakdown Lane

You'll find shoulders at the top of your back, not on the highways. What people in other parts of the country call the highway shoulder, people in Massachusetts call the Breakdown Lane because it does just that—provides a safe, paved place for people to pull over. If you're caught by a statie banging a uey on the pike, you'll have to pull over to the breakdown lane.

95/128/93/Route 1

No one has ever claimed that Boston and the surrounding areas are easy to navigate, but that is how you can tell who is from here and who isn't. The roadways all across the commonwealth have been built and rebuilt since the beginning of America. The roads are so confusing that you can be going south on one highway and north on another without even knowing it. Ask someone how to get to 128 and they may give you directions to 95 (or Route 1) and they are still sending you the right way. When it comes to roads, one thing Bostonians never do is put "The" in front of a highway number, save that for California!

Rotary

Most of Boston's, and New England's, roads were built before the automobile and had to adapt from the horse and buggy days. That said, our major intersections are a complete disaster. To conform to the growing number of cars, they put in rotaries. Not roundabouts, not traffic circles: rotaries. These circular nightmares allow people to enter from one road and exit onto another. Though often congested, the only real problems in the rotaries come from people who don't know what to do upon entering. If you find yourself in this situation, the rule is people in the rotary have right of way, so those entering must yield. It sounds easier than it actually is so really just say your pray-ahs and GO!

Statie

You've got your local police, Boston City police (BPD), then you've got your staties. Though most-often seen on highways like 128 and the Pike, they're in fact all over the state, all the time. You could take forever and call them state troopers, but Staties just makes the most sense. Whether they're local, BPD, or staties, they've proven to be some of the finest law enforcement this world has ever seen.

On a Boat, Under a Train, Car, and Plane

Built in 1928 and originally called the Cottage Farm Bridge, the now Boston University Bridge (BU Bridge) is the only place in America where you can sail on a boat, under a train that is driving under a car and under a plane. Yes, the double decker bridge has both car traffic and train traffic, over the Charles River in very close proximity to Logan Airport. The bridge connects Cambridge to Boston, mainly the BU campus, which is how it got its new name.

The T

The MBTA (Massachusetts Bay Transportation Authority), known in Boston as the T, is how most commuters get around the city and surrounding areas. The T has different lines that are distinguished by color. No matter which train you're taking, or how often it is supposed to run, chances are it is going to be late. Jokes aside, it was a huge feat to build such an intricate subway/rail system in such an old city.

The MBTA has four lines: the Red Line (built for the Harvard students whose color is crimson), the Blue Line (because it runs below the ocean), the Green (because it goes to the grass-filled outer suburbs), and Orange (because it ran above Orange Street). The newest addition is the Silver Line, which consists of buses that run from the Seaport to Logan International Airport. Though it is also not a subway, the Purple Line is the commuter rail which runs all around the eastern part of Massachusetts.

Whadjasay?

There are lots of words in Boston that will make non-Chowdaheads turn their heads and ask what you said. This section of the book will help you navigate all around the city without having to ask "whadjasay?" every five minutes.

Allston Christmas

Boston is home to over sixty colleges, so there are definitely some aspects of living that are dictated by students and make this city a "college town" for nine months of the year. September 1 kicks off the school year, and with it many leases are signed, apartments swapped, and people are moving all over. This process creates a mass amount of furniture, TVs, dishes, and other household items left on the roadside for the next generation of students. These new students have their taking of all these "new" items. The Allston neighborhood is the most popular amongst students so they have the most "gifts," so many in fact that September 1 has been dubbed "Allston Christmas."

Booted

If you choose to talk smack to a Yankee fan at the bar, chances are the bouncer or host will politely ask you to leave. This is what we call being "booted" from somewhere. Have one too many Sam Adams at Fenway and you're for sure going to be booted. You can also be booted from a taxi or Uber if the driver is afraid your Fenway Frank and chowdah is about to end up on his backseat.

Book It

After you've played a little ding-dong ditch on your neighbors, you better book it home before they see you and call your mothah! Not to be confused with the reading program that gets you free pizza at Pizza Hut, "Book It" is what we say when you need to get away fast—not kind of fast, wicked fast.

Lynn, Lynn the City of Sin

Whether you've been there or not, you've heard this song about Lynn, Massachusetts. The city north of Boston has been around since the industrial revolution but has always had the reputation as "The city of sin." When you say Lynn to a Massachusetts native, chances are he'll start chanting this poem:

Lynn, Lynn the city of sin, You never come out, the way you came in, You ask for water, but they give you gin, The girls say no, yet they always give in, If you're not bad, they won't let you in, It's the damndest city I've ever lived in, Lynn, Lynn the city of sin, you never come out, the way you came in.

Carriage

The things at the grocery store that no one puts away properly aren't called shopping carts, and they most certainly aren't called buggies; they're carriages. Not to be confused with what a horse pulls, these metal things will carry your food, kids, and even your toilet paper around the store, hence carriage.

Clickah

We all have tons of them; they always get lost; our parents can barely use them; they're the source of most marital and sibling fights alike. What are they? Your clickahs! Whoever has control of the clickah, controls what is on the TV and for how long. Some people call them a remote, but that's a word that describes an island in the Caribbean, so that's just weird.

Boston's Most Popular

Irregardless

This word ironically is used by Bostonians to make them, or the point they're trying to make, look smart and valid; however it's not really a word. Well technically it is a word, but not really because it makes no sense. Here is the officall response from dictionary.com:

"*Irregardless* is a nonstandard synonym for *regardless,* which means "without concern as to advice, warning, or hardship," or "heedless." Its nonstandard status is due to the double negative construction of the prefix *ir-* with the suffix -less. The prefix *ir-* means "not," while the suffix -less means "without," literally translating to "not without regard." This, of course, is the opposite of what English speakers generally intend to convey when using this term; for this reason, style guides unanimously urge against using *irregardless.*

Although editors purge *irregardless* from most published writing, the term is alive and well in spoken English and is recorded in most dictionaries. Those who use it may do so to add emphasis."

Irregardless of what the what those smart people say, it is still used all over the city.

Yous Guys

Now this term separates the people actually *from* Boston and people from the suburbs. Yous Guys is the northerner's version of "y'all," which means you all, or a bunch of people. This has most likely been the bane of every English teacher in Boston public schools since the beginning of time, but it's going to take a lot more than some grammar lessons to crack this. What do yous guys think?

Whaddup Ked

Much like the term, "Hawahyah," Whaddup Ked? is a salutation used in the streets of Boston that doesn't warrant a response, or can be replied to with, "Whaddup Ked?" It simply means, "How are you?" "What's going on?" Remember if you answer with how you actually are, or what's going on, you're just weird.

Diggah

A very common term in the sports world. When you fall wicked hard, you took a diggah! Whether you're running around a baseball field or sit too far back in your seat; if you fall, you took a diggah and will hear about it from your friends for days to come. Don't worry, even the best Boston athletes have taken diggahs and lived to tell about it.

Down Cellah

When you can't find something, chances are its down cellah. Whether you go down the kitchen stairs or through a bulkhead, you're in the cellah. Basements in Boston usually have nice carpeting and drywall while your cellar has your christmas decorations and your parents' old records.

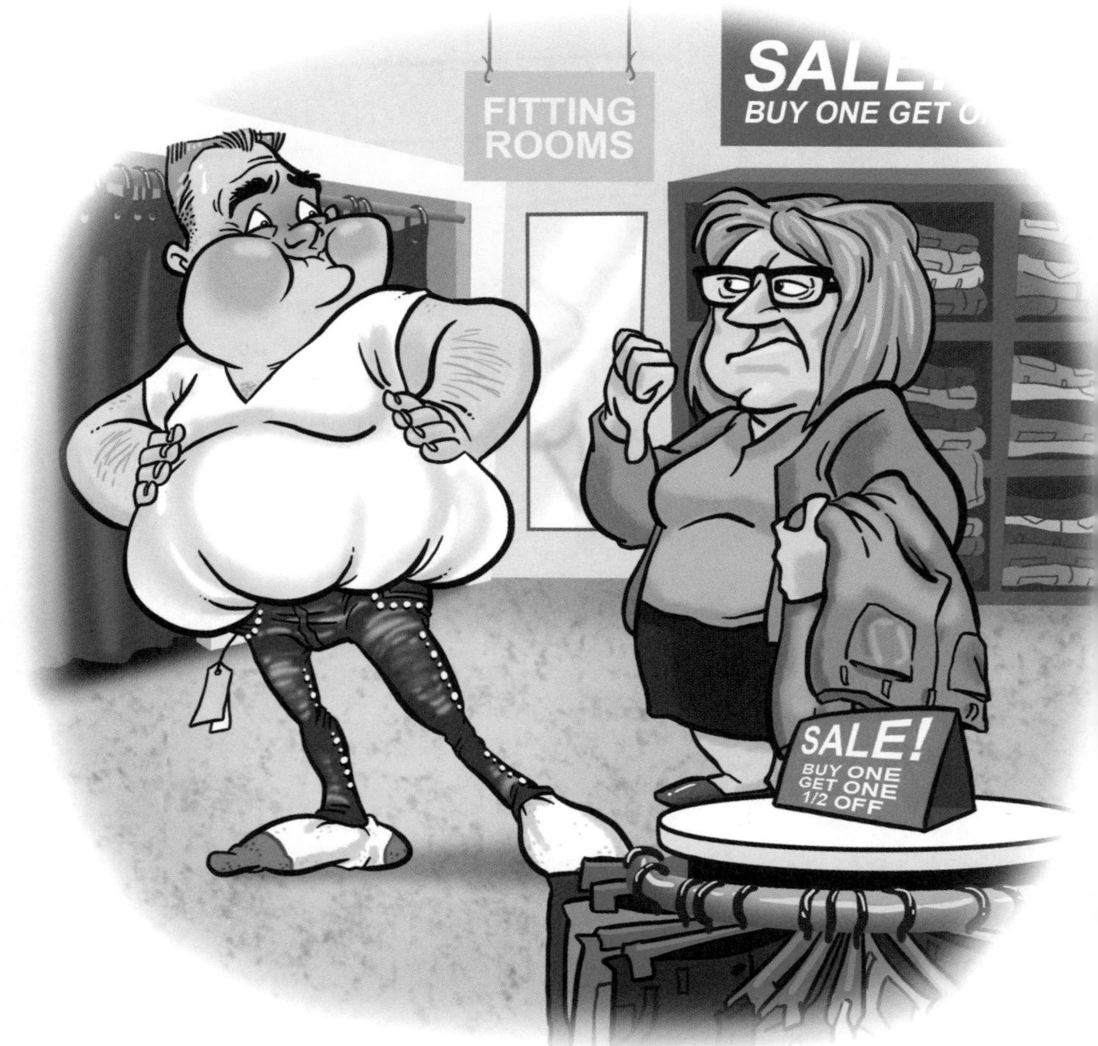
FITTING ROOMS
SALE!
BUY ONE GET O
SALE!
BUY ONE GET ONE 1/2 OFF

Dungarees

They're not jeans, or Levis; they're dungarees. Those denim pants you can wear with everything, and got yelled at for getting grass stains on, are dungarees. Whether pants or overalls, they're dungarees. No ifs, ands, or buts about it. Growing up you most likely got a pair of dungarees for school and another for play—most likely both were from Jordan Marsh or Filene's.

Elastic

The stretchy things that are used to keep small things together and your newspaper folded aren't called rubber bands, they're called elastics. If someone asks for a rubber band, they're clearly from out of town.

Light Dawns Over Marble Head

When you were sitting in a high school class and finally had a "light bulb moment," you probably had a teacher say, "Aaaah a light dawns over Maaaarble Head." Marblehead is a seaside town on the eastern tip of Massachusetts, so it sees the sunrise before a lot of the rest of the state; however this expression uses Marble Head as two words; inferring that the person is dense, or less than smart.

Hawahyah

Much like Hawaii has "Aloha," Boston has "hawahyah?" This is what you say to your neighbor in the morning or someone you make eye contact with in the store. But if someone says it to you, you certainly do NOT tell them how you actually are. You simply reply with, "Hawahyah?" (all one word). This is not an invitation to spill all your problems to a complete stranger, it is a simple way to acknowledge them, and them you.

SER EYE
SURGERY
CALL
TODAY!
1-800-555-LAZR
LIMITED TIME OFFER!
* will NOT give you the ability to shoot lasers from your eyes
LEARN to
ENGLISH REAL
GOOD 1-800-555-YAPP
HAIWAHYAH?

Howl

If you tell a joke that's kind of funny then people will laugh, but if you tell a joke that's wicked funny, people are going to howl! You haven't really made your friends' day until you hear them howling at some joke you told earlier in the day.

Huckaloogie

In Boston one doesn't simply spit, you huck a loogie or huckaloogie. Though your mother hates it, she knows you do it. It probably makes you the cool kid in the schoolyahd; just don't do it front of your grandparents.

Brahmin

Boston Brahmins was an aristocratic society in Boston made up of a few families, including landowners and politicians. It was believed they were closer to God, and that certain families were second only to him. The families ran in the same circles, sending their kids to the same schools and often marrying their children off amongst each other. It was quite ironic that America was founded on the abolishment of aristocracy, but quickly implemented a similar class system to which they were accustomed. Though the family names are still popular in Boston, the families are not held to the same regard as they were in the past. Much of their wealth still dates back to an origin of shipping and other things from the American Revolution.

In Town

When Bostonians hear "the city" they assume you're talking about New York City. When you are going into Boston for the night, or even heading downtown from an outlying neighborhood, you're going "In Town." There's no real origin as to why, and it isn't as popular as it once was, but to most Boston natives, there is a clear distinction between "The City" and "Town."

No Suh

When you get wicked excited in Boston and can't believe something happened, it's completely normal to shout "no suh" to express such belief. Though often thought to be said by girls, guys are also known to have an instinctive "no suh" in them every once in while, whether they want to believe it or not . . . yes suh!

Packie Run

Before every party and barbeque someone's gotta do it, and you better make sure your beer or handle is on the list. I'm talking about a packie run. Other places around the world would ask if you "want something at the liquor store." In Boston, we say "Tom's runnin a packie, whadya want?!" This has to do with the fact that our liquor stores are called package stores and thus "packie" was born.

The twenty-first Amendment repealed prohibition and allowed the sale of alcohol again in 1933; however Massachusetts still has wicked weird Puritanic blue laws that dictate how and when we can buy alcohol. One of these laws prohibits grocery stores from selling liquor and requires it only be sold at a package store aka a packie. Package stores weren't allowed to sell liquor on Sunday until as recently as 2004 when the law allowed them to open at noon. The law was modified in 2014 allowing them to open at 10 a.m..

Though the laws are evolving with time, it's unlikely that package stores will go away anytime soon. Since Massachusetts is a commonwealth, it tries to keep as many jobs and businesses open as possible. Allowing big box grocers to sell alcohol would eliminate many private small businesses. Long live the packie run!

Pahlah

When people hear the word "parlor," they often think of a massage place, or a room in a funeral home. In Boston, it is the front room of a house that you're only allowed to sit in on holidays and absolutely without sneakers or dungarees on. Whether you have a triple deckah in Southie or a mansion up the North Shore, chances are you've got a pahlah that your mom rarely lets you sit in.

Pockabook

Often called a purse, handbag, or just a bag in other places; we call it a pockabook. It's where a lady keeps all her personal things, not excluding her boyfriend's keys and wallet during a night out or trip the Square One Mall. Whether it's Coach, Louis Vuitton, or from the bargain bin at Filene's, it's still a pockabook.

Rubbish

That thing you have to take out as a kid for a measly allowance and put on the street once a week isn't trash, it's rubbish. The term originated in England and migrated to New England, but didn't make it much farther. You throw your rubbish in a barrel.

Sneakahs

Let's get something straight, tennis shoes are for playing tennis! Nobody in Boston wears tennis shoes unless they are on a court with a racket, a net, and yellow ball. Shoes are what you wear to a fancy party or nightclub. Sneakers, or as we call them "sneakahs" or sometimes just "sneaks" are the things that go on your feet on a daily basis.

Many people don't know that Boston is actually a hotbed for sneaker companies. Puma, Converse, New Balance, Reebok, Saucony, and Sperry Topsider are all headquartered in the Boston area. So don't tell us what to call the things that we play such a part in making!

Space Saver

It's common practice in Boston for people to save their parking spots with anything from trash barrels to Dunkin Donuts billboards. There is no official rule on the books, but the "Menino Rule" from Mayor Thomas Menino's days in office is that you could save your spot for up to forty-eight hours after the parking ban is lifted. People don't always abide by that however.

Although Boston is known for its friendly neighborhoods and helpful residents, that is all out the window when it comes to parking spots. There are stories of cars' tires being slashed, paint being thrown on them, or the ever-popular being shoveled back in. Meaning if someone takes your spot, you simply spend your time and energy putting the snow back around them so they have to earn that spot.

I have lived in Boston for five years and know the rules of my neighborhood; however I've also had my spot stolen. I am not a malicious person but I am also not a quiet person, so I did leave a (waterproof) note for the culprit. The spot was later vacated and I had it back. When it was initially taken, I had three different people call me at work to tell me someone had stolen it—how neighborly!

Strollah

We've already established that a carriage is what you have at DeMoula's to get your groceries, but a strollah is what you push your baby around in. It's always confusing when other people say they took their kid for a walk in a carriage but even more weird when they say pram. Carriage = groceries, strollah = baby, get it?

Triple Deckah

These three-story apartment buildings adorn the streets of Boston and can be found in almost every neighborhood. They are usually light-framed wood construction with each floor consisting of a single apartment, although it is not uncommon to have two apartments on one floor.

They became popular between 1870 and 1920 and appealed to both landlords and immigrant families. It is a way for a landlord to live in one apartment while collecting rent from the other two. Also, many extended families occupy them and move between apartments as life changes. Grandparents will move from the family apartment upstairs to a lower apartment so their kids can now raise their kids in the bigger "family" apartment.

With the change in demographics and influx of urban housing, many triple deckers are being turned into individually owned condos; meaning there are multiple owners of what was once an income property.

Trot Trot to Boston

No matter where you grew up in Massachusetts, whether you remember it or not, someone in your family bounced you on their knee and sang "Trot Trot to Boston" or some variation thereof to entertain you. A popular way to (easily) entertain infants is to chant this poem while they bounce up and down on your lap, ultimately "falling" between your legs. "Trot Trot to Boston, Trot Trot to Lynn; Look out little (baby's name), you might fall in!"

Variety Store

Often called a "five and dime" or a bodega, variety stores are more than a convenience store, but less than a department store. They are those places that have everything. They have food products to clothing products. They often offer things at a set price as in "everything for a dollar." They are located all over Boston and the name is funny to most people from out of town.

Charlie Card

When the MBTA, or the T, implemented smart cards for people to pay fares on subway and eliminate the token system, there was only one "person" that it could be named after: a fictitious character named Charlie. Charlie was the topic of the mayoral election in 1949 and is believed to be "forever 'neath the streets of Boston."

In 1949, the Massachusetts legislation proposed that T riders would have to pay a dime to get on the subway and a nickel to get off. This sounded preposterous to many people, especially mayoral candidate Walter O'Brien. O'Brien painted the scene of a man only having enough money to get on the T, and not enough to get off. So he said that his wife would have to go bring him a sandwich every day and pass it on the train for him to eat.

O'Brien lost the election but not without leaving his mark on Boston's pop culture. A song was written for Charlie called "MTA" and is still performed in bars and coffee shops around the city. So next time you swipe your Charlie Card (for well over a dime), think of these lyrics:

Let me tell you the story
Of a man named Charlie
On a tragic and fateful day
He put ten cents in his pocket,
Kissed his wife and family
Went to ride on the MTA
Charlie handed in his dime
At the Kendall Square Station
And he changed for Jamaica Plain

When he got there the conductor
  told him,
"One more nickel."
Charlie could not get off that train.

Chorus:
Did he ever return,
No he never returned
And his fate is still unlearn'd
He may ride forever

'neath the streets of Boston
He's the man who never returned.

ChahlieCahd

...husetts Bay Transportation Authority

Now all night long
Charlie rides through the tunnels
  the station
Saying, "What will become of me?
Crying
How can I afford to see
My sister in Chelsea
Or my cousin in Roxbury?"
Charlie's wife goes down
To the Scollay Square station
Every day at quarter past two
And through the open window

She hands Charlie a sandwich
As the train comes rumblin' through.
As his train rolled on
underneath Greater Boston
Charlie looked around and sighed:
"Well, I'm sore and disgusted
And I'm absolutely busted;
I guess this is my last long ride."
{this entire verse was replaced by a
  banjo solo}
Now you citizens of Boston,
Don't you think it's a scandal
That the people have to pay and pay
Vote for Walter A. O'Brien
Fight the fare increase!
And fight the fare increase
Vote for Walter O'Brien!
Get poor Charlie off the MTA.

Chorus:
Or else he'll never return,
No he'll never return
And his fate will be unlearned
He may ride forever
'neath the streets of Boston
He's the man (Who's the man)
He's the man who never returned.
He's the man (Oh, the man)
He's the man who never returned.
He's the man who never returned.

Whiffle

When the weather starts warming up in New England and Wiffle balls and bats come out to play, boys all over are getting another kind of whiffle. Often in the same backyard from their father or brothers they're getting their buzz cut for the summah, which is called a whiffle. Go into any barber shop in Boston and ask for a whiffle, you'll get all the wintah hair shaved off and be ready for summah!

Wicked

When someone in Boston says "wicked" they aren't talking about a witch and they certainly aren't talking about a Broadway musical. Wicked is the word we use to describe anything we are excited about. Other people might say "really," "very," or the worst word ever, "hella." Though the English dictionary would say wicked is an adjective because it's used as a description word, in Boston it is an adverb because it's used to enhance the description word. Examples: "My chowdah is wicked hot." "Dunks was wicked crowded this morning."

Sports

If you are from Boston there are two things you need to survive your day, underpants (to avoid being arrested) and a way to stay connected to "The Sox, Pats, B's & C's." Boston is no doubt the greatest sports town in America, we live and breathe it all day long. Ask someone from Boston how they are feeling today and you might get this answer: "Good, the Sox won last night."

The Beanpot

Contrary to how it reads, "The Beanpot" is not a big vat of baked beans that you would devour and have a few bad days on the potty. It's a hockey tournament that features the four major hockey college teams in the Boston area. Boston University, Northeastern, Harvard, and Boston College battle to raise the coveted "Beanpot" trophy in early February at "The Garden" (see page 181). Crazy college students and hockey fan locals treat this event with great importance and excitement, as it gives bragging rights over your cross-town rivals. Dress warm because it can be "wicked cold" inside the rink!

Bruins

The Boston Bruins a.k.a "The Bs" are the meat and potatoes of Boston sports. The rough and tumble sport of hockey has a cult following and those who call themselves "Bs" fans do it with a mix of passion, history, and pride flowing through them.

The Celtics

The Boston Celtics are to Boston like a foundation is to a house. They are the rock of Boston sports. Their success and history runs deep within the culture and soul of Boston. Their logo is a shamrock symbol that many have tattooed to various places on their bodies. The "C's" have been in the NBA since 1946 and they have more championships than any other team. They are considered one of the most successful sports franchises ever.

The Garden

When people outside Boston hear "I am heading to The Garden," they probably assume you are out planting perennials, daffodils, and maybe tomatoes. However, "The Garden" to locals is the place where the Bruins and Celtics play. They can tear the stadium down; rename it with some corporate pre-fix; paint it tan, green, orange, black, or whatever, but it will always be known as simply "The Garden."

Gillette Stadium

In short this is the stadium where the New England Patriots play. Just as with "The Garden," there is pushback on a brand monopolizing the name of a stadium. We would typically change it to something else and ignore the corporate namesake, but Gillette as a company has a lot of history in Boston so we give this one a pass.

Head of the Charles

The Head of The Charles Regatta, also known as HOCR, is a rowing head race held on the penultimate complete weekend of October (i.e., on the Saturday that falls between the 17 and the 23 of the month, and on the Sunday immediately afterward) each year on the Charles River, which separates Boston and Cambridge. The Regatta attracts thousands of rowers and spectators to the bank of the river.

New England Revolution

Soccer games have enthusiastic, fun fans. Most Rev fans don't even care if a game ends in a tie after 5 hours (and most of them do). All of our soccer games growing up were ties—or at least that's what they told us.

Marathon Monday

The day of the Marathon in Boston is a nostalgic day in the city. Not because everyone in Boston has much interest in who wins the race, but it's a gathering of support and love around town. Cheering on runners who are enduring pain and sacrifice to support different causes is inspiring and invigorating for all involved. On top of this, the Sox play an early day game, some local colleges cancel classes, and pretty much everyone has consumed some adult beverage by the time the race has finished. It's quite an eventful and prideful day in Boston, many say it's the best day of the year in town.

It's also a day to honor the victims and families of the 2013 bombings. As Bostonians though we refuse to let terrorism and violence change our way of life.

The Patriots

The New England Patriots have a love like no other. "Pats" fans would line up shoulder to shoulder with muskets in their hands if it meant protecting Patriot Nation.

Red Sox & Fenway Park

To most people in Boston the Red Sox or "The Sox" are like another family member. They are a part of your life, always on your mind, sometimes you love them, and sometimes they can ruin your day. A diehard fan will either go to bed happy or angry depending on how the game went that day.

They have been a part of the city for over one hundred years and have been playing at Fenway Park since 1912.

Index

30 Rack, 45
95/128/93/Route 1, 99

Allston Christmas, 110

Back Bay, The, 18
Badaydahs, 50
Bang a Uey, 88
Bay State, 37
Beacon Hill, 18
Beanpot, The, 174
Beatah, 91
Big Dig, 92
Blinkahs, 95
Blizzard of 78, 11
Book It, 114
Booted, 113
Boston Common, 23
Boston Gas Tank, 24
Brahmin, 141
Breakdown Lane, 96
Bruins, 177
Bubblah, 53

Carriage, 118
Celtics, The, 178
Charlestown, 18
Charlie Card, 166
Chowdah, 54
Clickah, 121
Cod, 61

Commonwealth, 14
Cranberries, 62
Cuppah Regulah, 57

Diggah, 125
Dinner vs Supper, 85
Dorchester, 19
Down the Cape, 38
Dungarees, 129
Dunks, 58

East Boston, 19
Elastic, 130

Faneuil Hall, 27
Fenway Park, 192
Fluff, 49
Foliage, 2
Franks and Beans, 65
Frappe, 46

Garden, The, 181
Gillette Stadium, 182

Hancock Tower, 29
Hawahyah, 134
Haymarket, 30
Head of the Charles, 185
Heat Wave, 2
Hoodsie, 66
Howl, 137
Hub, The, 33
Huckaloogie, 138

Indian Summah, 5
In Town, 142
Italian Ice, 69

Jamaica Plain, 19
Jimmies, 70

Keggah, 44
Kicked, 44

Leaf Peepahs, 2
Light Dawns Over Marble Head, 133
Lobstah Roll, 73
Lynn Lynn City of Sin, 117

Marathon Monday, 189
Marblehead, 133
Market basket, 74
Martha's Vineyard, 38
Muggy, 5

Nantucket, 38
Necco, 77
Neighborhood, 17
Newbury Street, 34
New England Boiled Dinnah, 82
New England Revolution, 186
No Name Storm, 6
Nor' Eastah, 6
North End, 19
No Suh, 145

Packie Run, 146
Pahdee Plattah, 78

Pahlah, 149
Patriots, The, 190
Plastahed, 45
Pockabook, 150

Red Sox, 192
Rotary, 100
Rozzie, 20
Rubbish, 153

Scorchah, 9
Sneakahs, 154
South End, 20
Southie, 20
Space Saver, 157
Statie, 103
Strollah, 158
Sub, 78
Tonic, 81
Triple Deckah, 161
Trot Trot, 162
T, The, 107

Variety Store, 165

Whaddup Ked, 123
Whiffle, 168
Wicked, 171
Wintah, 10

Yous Guys, 122

ZooMass, 21

About the Authors

Ryan Gormady and Ryan DeLisle were both raised in the Boston area. They attended the University of Massachusetts together where they noticed that anyone from out of state had no idea what a "Bubblah" was.

Ryan DeLisle lived in Hawaii for a few years and began to appreciate the "funny" way he said things and took pride in friendly ridicule.

Ryan Gormady founded Chowaheadz, a company that sells Boston-themed products. They are close friends who smile every time they hear someone order a "quatah pounda shahp cheddah" at the deli.

About the Illustrator

Kevin Mulkern has been drawing since he was a young child with no athletic ability to speak of. Born and raised near Boston, his accent is so thick even locals give him a hard time about it.

About Chowdaheadz

Since 2003 Chowdaheadz has been creating lifestyle products that celebrate our love for Boston. Products are sold through the website and to select retailers in the Boston area. From t-shirts bearing the slogan "Wicked Pissah" to a candle called "Summahtime," the products are unique, fun, and designed for people who love Boston!

www.chowdaheadz.com